BREAKFAST

Easy To Learn Cartoon Prompts

A Generative AI Art Done For You Prompt Guide for Beginners

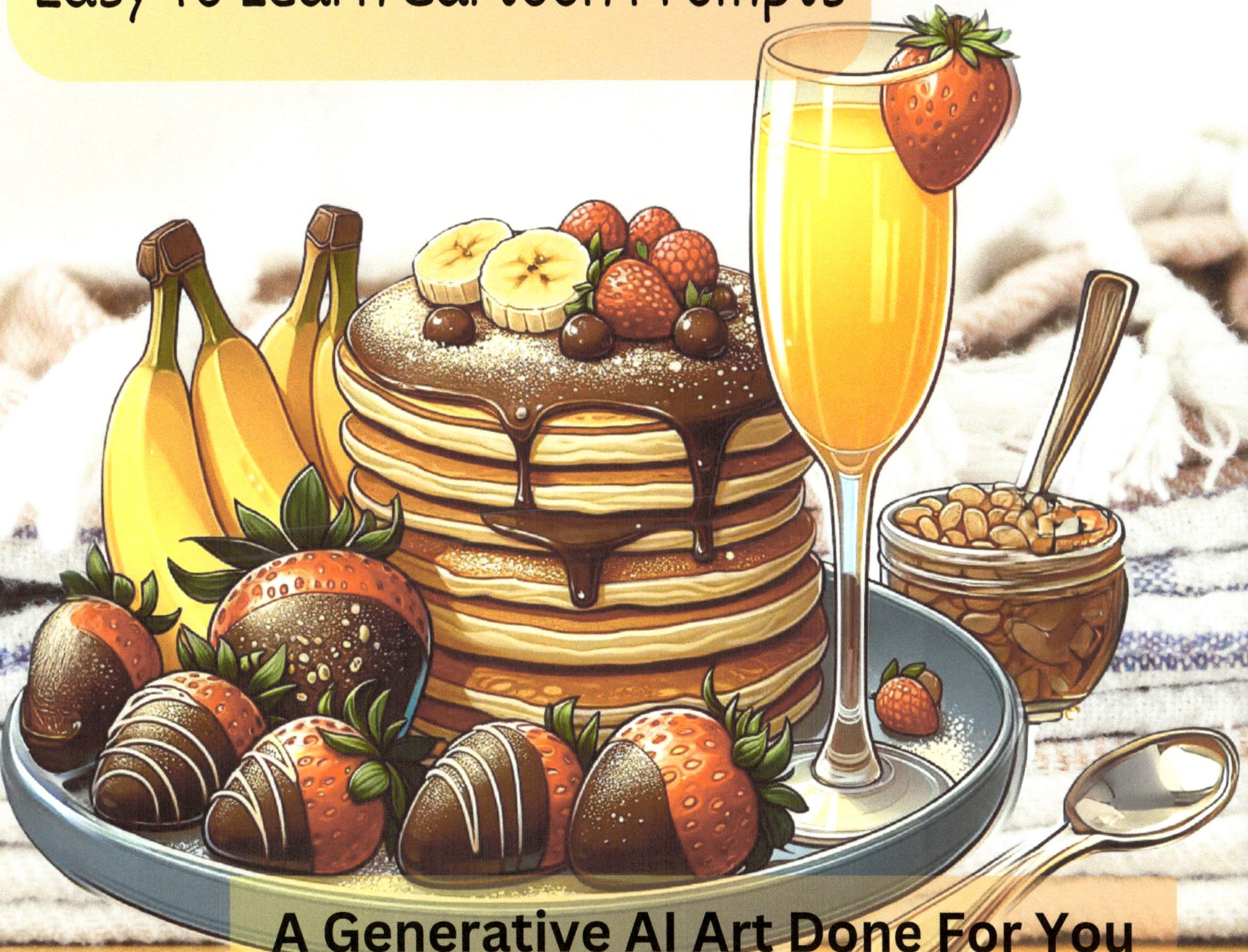

COVER PROMPT

Create a cartoon digital illustration of a brunch plate featuring chocolate-covered strawberries and bananas alongside whole grain fluffy pancakes. Accompany this delightful arrangement with a glass of mimosa, creating a perfect Sunday brunch setting. The illustration should capture a cozy and luxurious atmosphere, highlighting the rich colors and appealing textures of the chocolate-covered fruits and the whole grain pancakes. The style should be playful and charming, effectively conveying the essence of a leisurely and indulgent brunch experience with a touch of elegance provided by the mimosa.

Creating AI-generated images using prompts is a fascinating and accessible way for beginners to explore the capabilities of artificial intelligence in the realm of digital art. The process involves providing a detailed, written description or 'prompt' to an AI tool, which then interprets and translates these instructions into a visual representation. When crafting prompts, clarity and specificity are key; the more detailed the description, the closer the resulting image will align with your vision. For instance, specifying elements like setting, colors, mood, and subjects helps guide the AI. It's also important to experiment and iterate, as AI interpretations can vary widely based on the input. This process opens up a world of creative possibilities, allowing even those without traditional art skills to bring their imaginative concepts to life visually.

The following breakfast-related prompts are focused on creating images of various cartoon breakfast options. Each prompt was carefully crafted to highlight the technique of creating a breakfast's unique characteristics, showcasing its beauty and detail.

This prompt guide was designed to help you get started with using AI to bring to life a common food experience. Remember, you can take these prompts into an AI text tool and request additional based on the prompt you use.

While you can create additional prompts using a text based AI program, keep in mind you will need an art AI tool to create images. An example of this may be a paid program like ChatGPT DALL E3 or Midjourney and there are some free generative art programs as well. Check online for free platforms because this changes regularly. Contact us at hello@girlsandfinance with questions.

PROMPTS IN THIS GUIDE ARE FOR REFERENCE. RENDEREED ART WILL VARY.

HOW TO USE THE GUIDE:

1) DOWNLOAD TO YOUR DESKTOP OR SMART DEVICE, 2) COPY A PROMPT, 3) PASTE IT INTO CHATGPT WITH THE DALLE3 OPTION SELECTED, 4) DOWNLOAD YOUR ART AND USE IT OR 5) SELL IT AS STICKERS, JOURNAL COVERS AND MORE.

Oh how fun it is waking up everyday to a new experience awaiting - breakfast!

~ K. White

PROMPT

Create a cartoon digital illustration of a Sunday brunch plate featuring a lobster tail with the meat visible, an omelette, and a crepe as the main items. Add a side of fresh fruit to enhance the brunch experience. The setting should be luxurious and inviting, capturing the essence of a special seafood brunch. The illustration style should be playful yet sophisticated, highlighting the gourmet delight of the lobster tail, the richness of the omelette, and the sweetness of the crepe, all complemented by the freshness of the fruit.

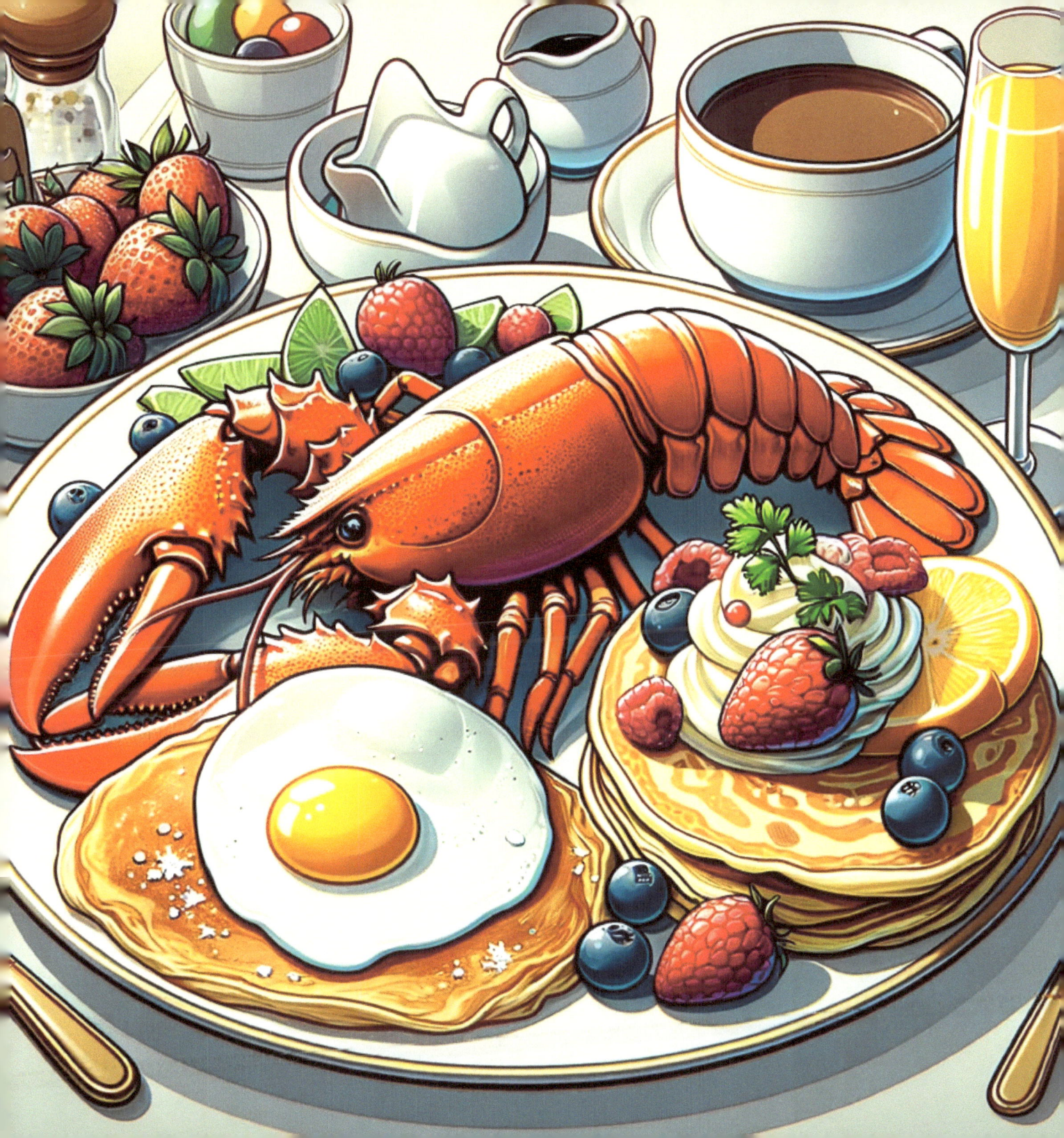

PROMPT

Create a cartoon digital illustration of a Sunday brunch plate featuring turkey sausage as the main item, served alongside fluffy pancakes and a fruit salad. The setting is cozy and inviting, perfectly embodying a family-friendly Sunday brunch atmosphere. The illustration style should be playful and charming, highlighting the essence of a comforting and delightful Sunday brunch with turkey sausage as a nutritious and tasty choice.

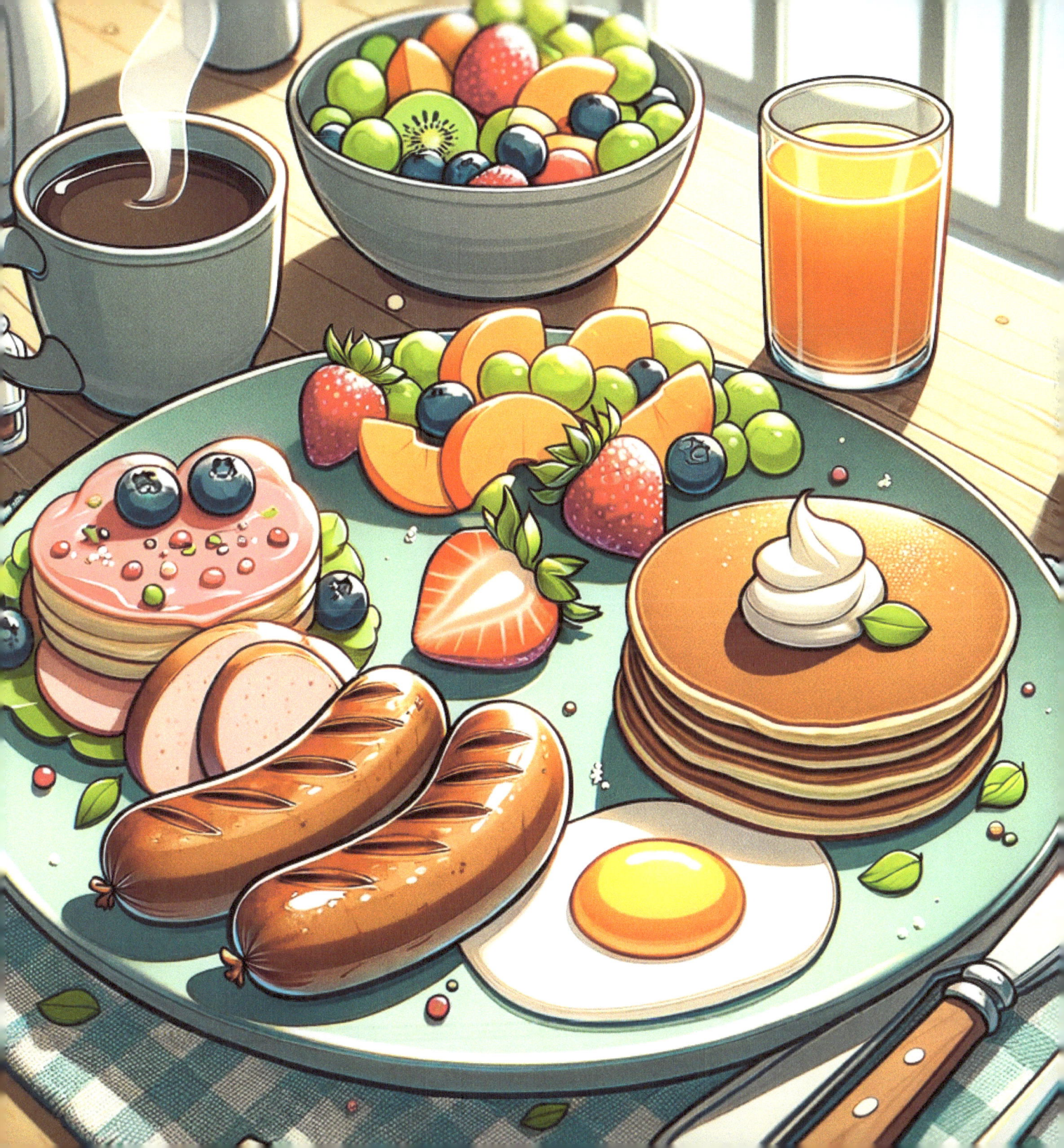

PROMPT

Create a cartoon digital illustration of a Sunday brunch plate featuring baked salmon as the main item, elegantly served with a side of cream cheese bagels and fresh avocado slices. The setting is festive and warm, showcasing a delightful Sunday brunch atmosphere with a variety of complementary breakfast dishes. The illustration style is playful and charming, perfectly capturing the essence of a savory and elegant Sunday brunch experience.

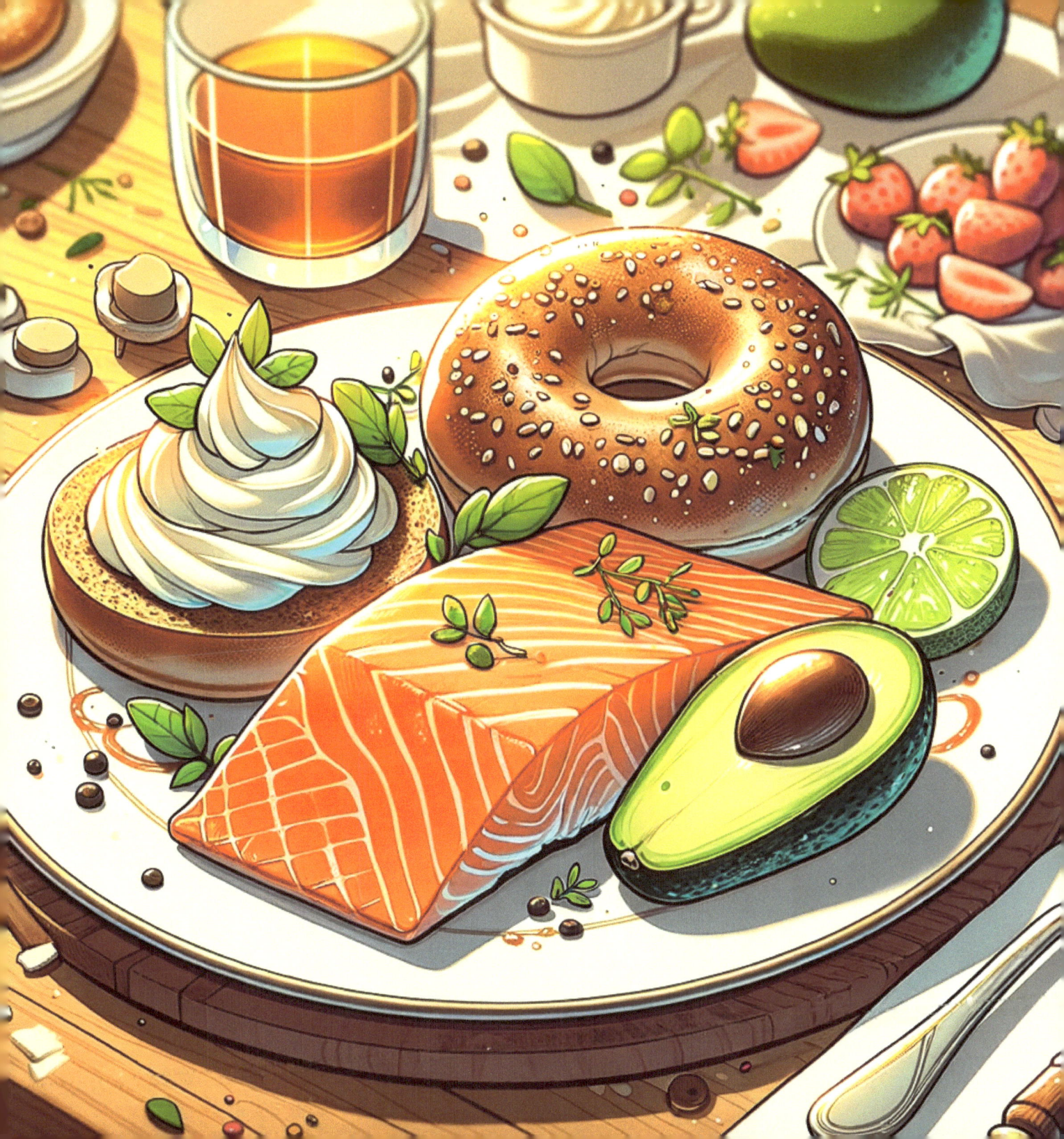

PROMPT

Create a cartoon digital illustration of a Sunday brunch plate featuring crispy fried green tomatoes as the main item, accompanied by complementary breakfast dishes like scrambled eggs and toast. The setting is festive and warm, capturing the essence of a delightful Sunday brunch with a variety of complimentary breakfast dishes to enhance the main item. The illustration style is playful and charming.

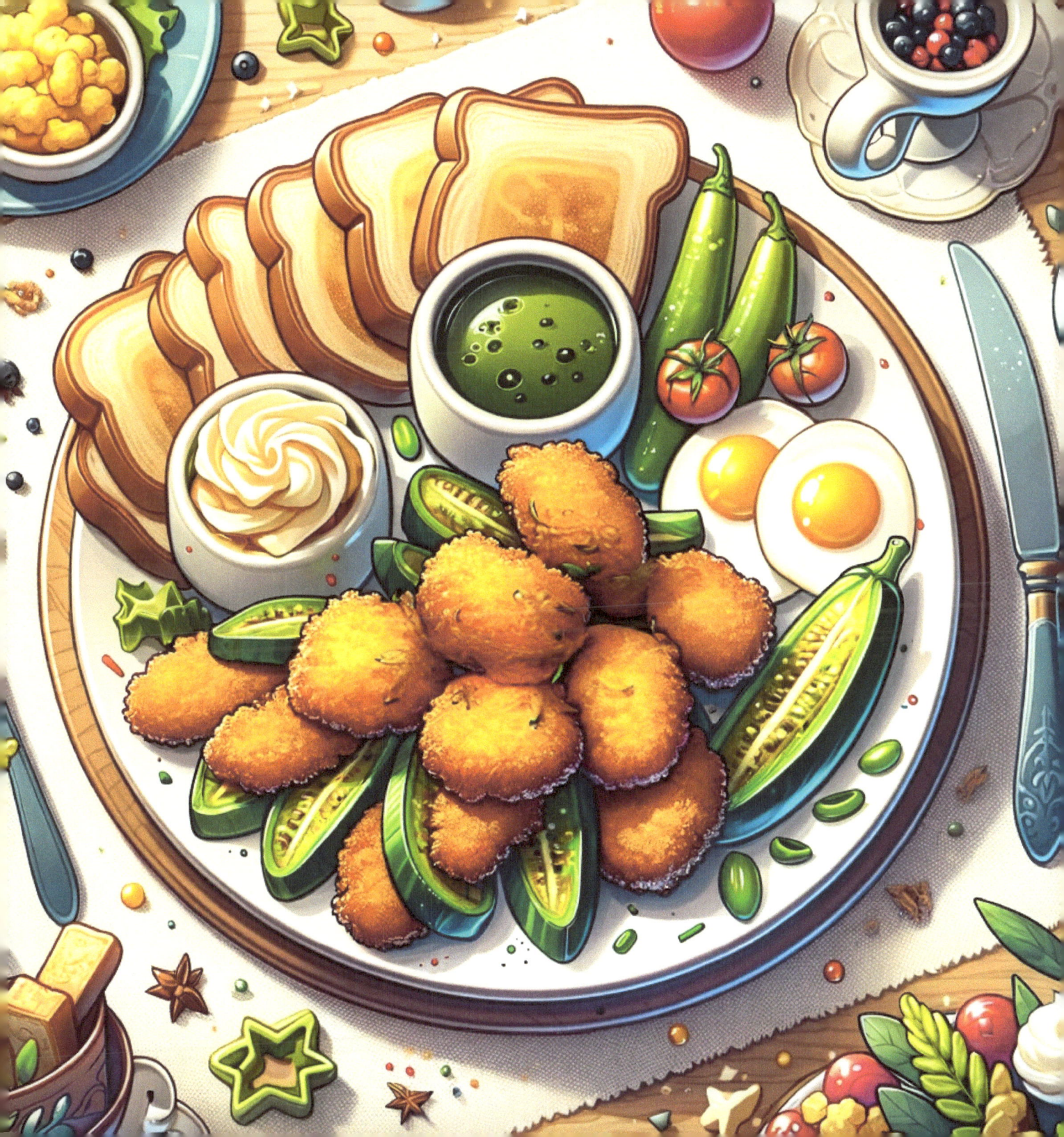

PROMPT

Create a cartoon digital illustration of a Sunday brunch plate with chicken tenders and grain waffles. The plate should display crispy fried chicken tenders paired with grain waffles, generously drizzled with maple syrup. Include a glass of orange juice and a cup of steaming coffee as accompaniments. Add a festive and romantic Sunday theme to the scene, including a small bowl of oatmeal on the side to complete the brunch setting. The illustration style should be playful and charming, designed to capture the essence of a hearty and delightful Sunday brunch. The overall composition should convey the joy and comfort of enjoying a beloved meal, making it visually appealing and inviting with the chicken tenders and grain waffles as the centerpiece.

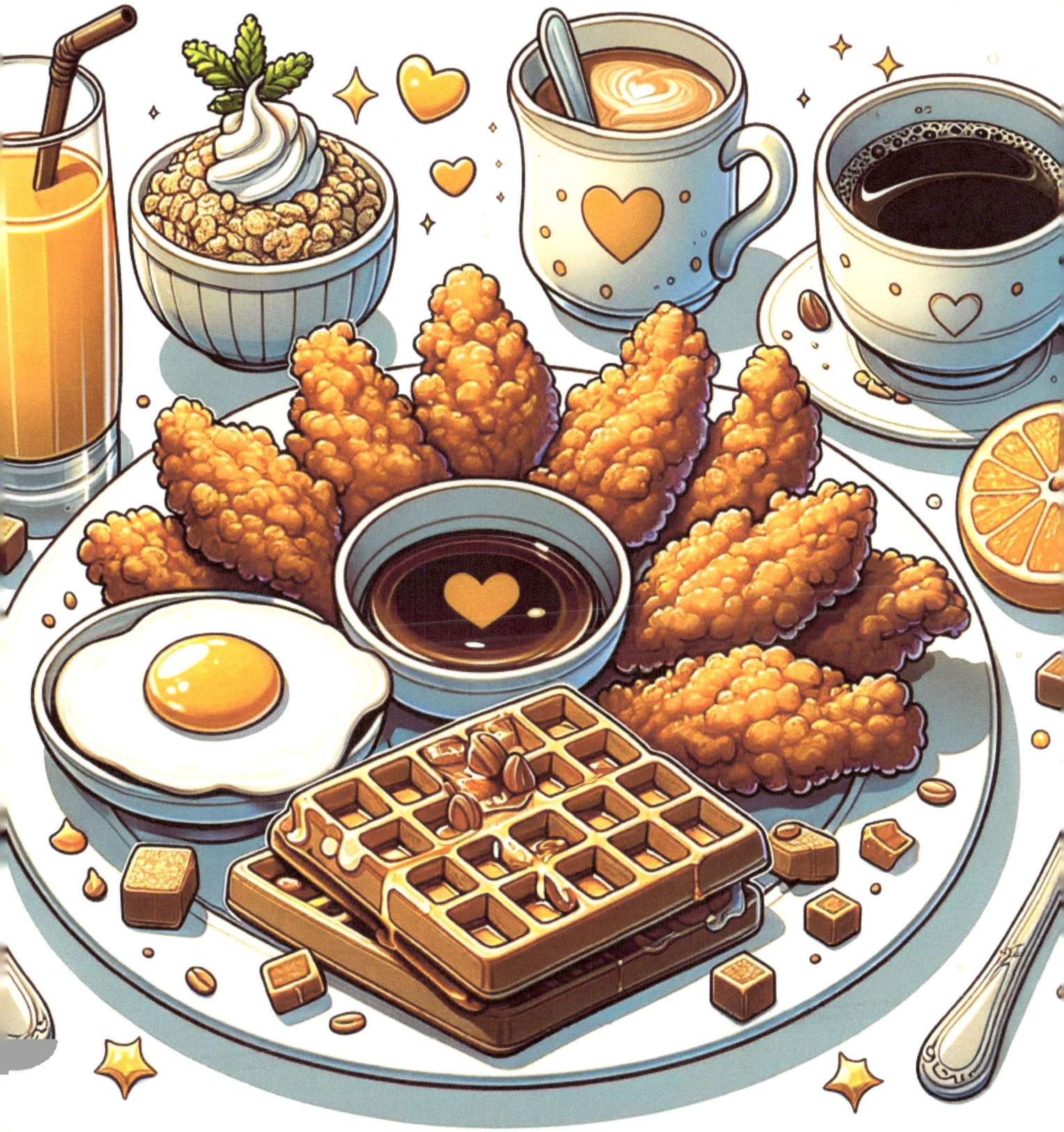

PROMPT

Create a cartoon digital illustration of a Sunday brunch plate with shrimp and grits. The plate should showcase creamy grits topped with juicy, seasoned shrimp, garnished with fresh herbs and a sprinkle of cheese. Include a small plate of fruit, a glass of pineapple juice, and a cup of steaming coffee as accompaniments. The setting is festive and warm, with a heartwarming theme, enhanced by small garnish around the plate. The illustration style is playful and charming, aimed at capturing the essence of a savory and delightful Sunday brunch. The overall composition should convey the joy and comfort of a leisurely Sunday morning, making it visually appealing and inviting with shrimp and grits as the centerpiece.

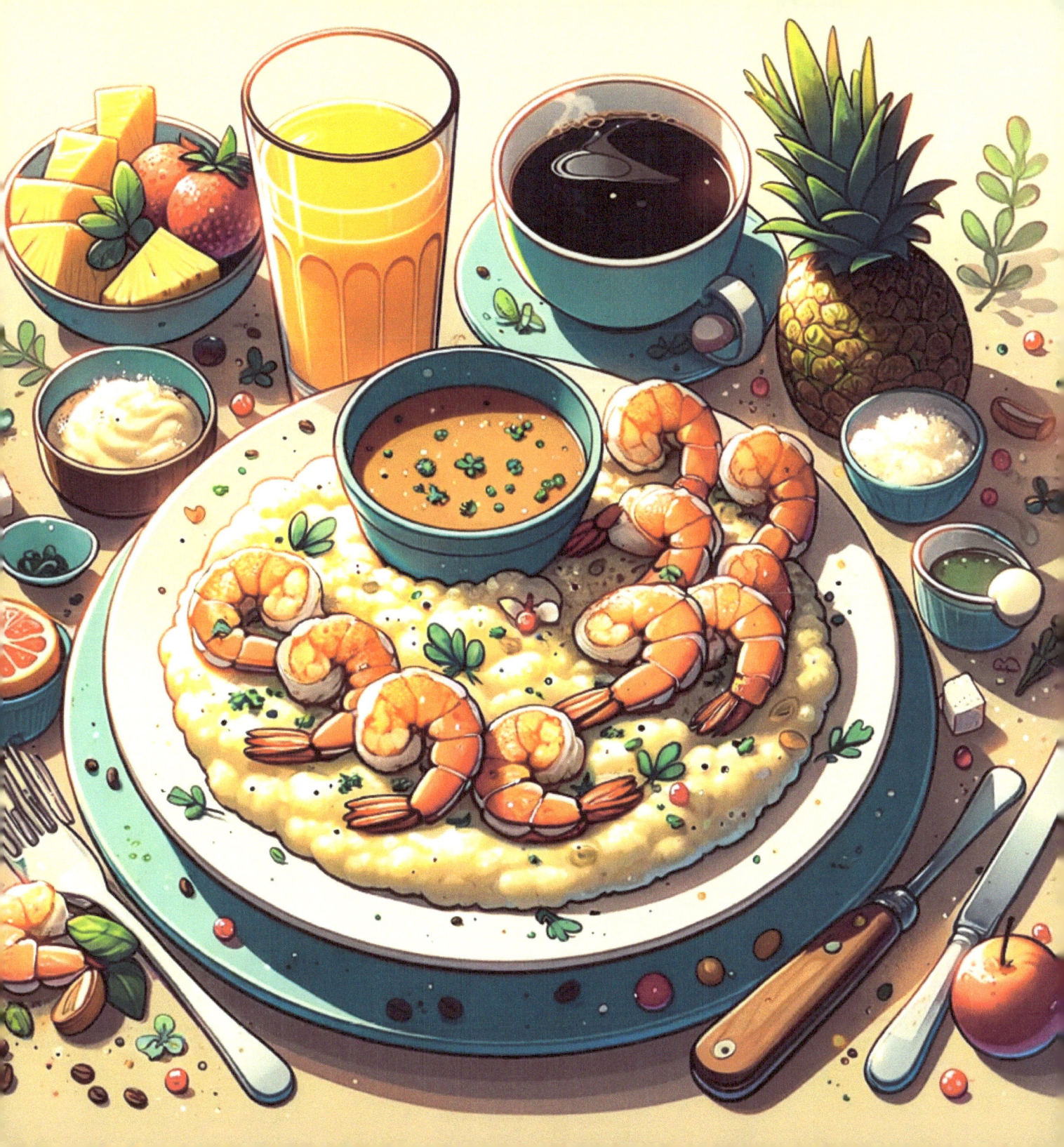

Create a cartoon digital illustration of a Sunday brunch plate featuring stacked French toast and perfectly cooked bacon. Include a glass of orange juice and a cup of steaming coffee as accompaniments. The plate should also be adorned with various brunch fixings like slices of fresh fruit, a small bowl of berries, and a generous drizzle of maple syrup over the French toast. The setting is festive and playful, with a heartwarming theme, highlighted by small decorative cookies around the plate. The illustration style should be playful and charming, aimed at capturing the essence of a delightful Sunday brunch, making it visually appealing and inviting, with French toast and bacon as the stars of the meal.

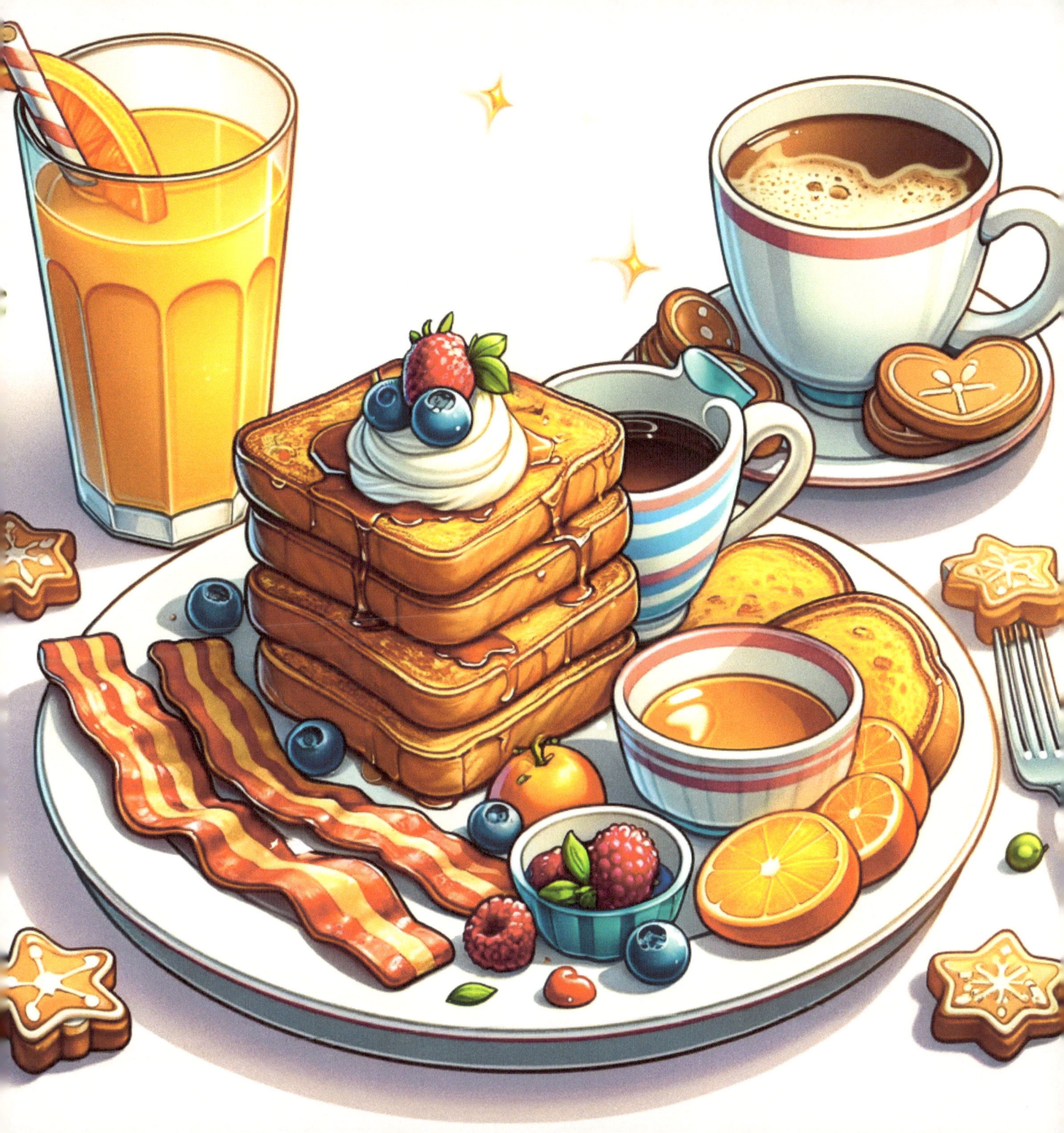

PROMPT

Create a cartoon digital illustration of a Sunday brunch plate without any text, featuring ham and fluffy scrambled eggs. The plate should showcase a generous serving of sliced ham alongside a mound of soft, fluffy scrambled eggs. Include a glass of orange juice and a cup of steaming coffee as accompaniments. The setting should be festive and romantic, with a playful theme, but without any decorative sugar or text around the plate. Maintain the playful and charming illustration style to capture the essence of a hearty and delightful Sunday brunch, emphasizing the warmth and joy of a leisurely Sunday morning.

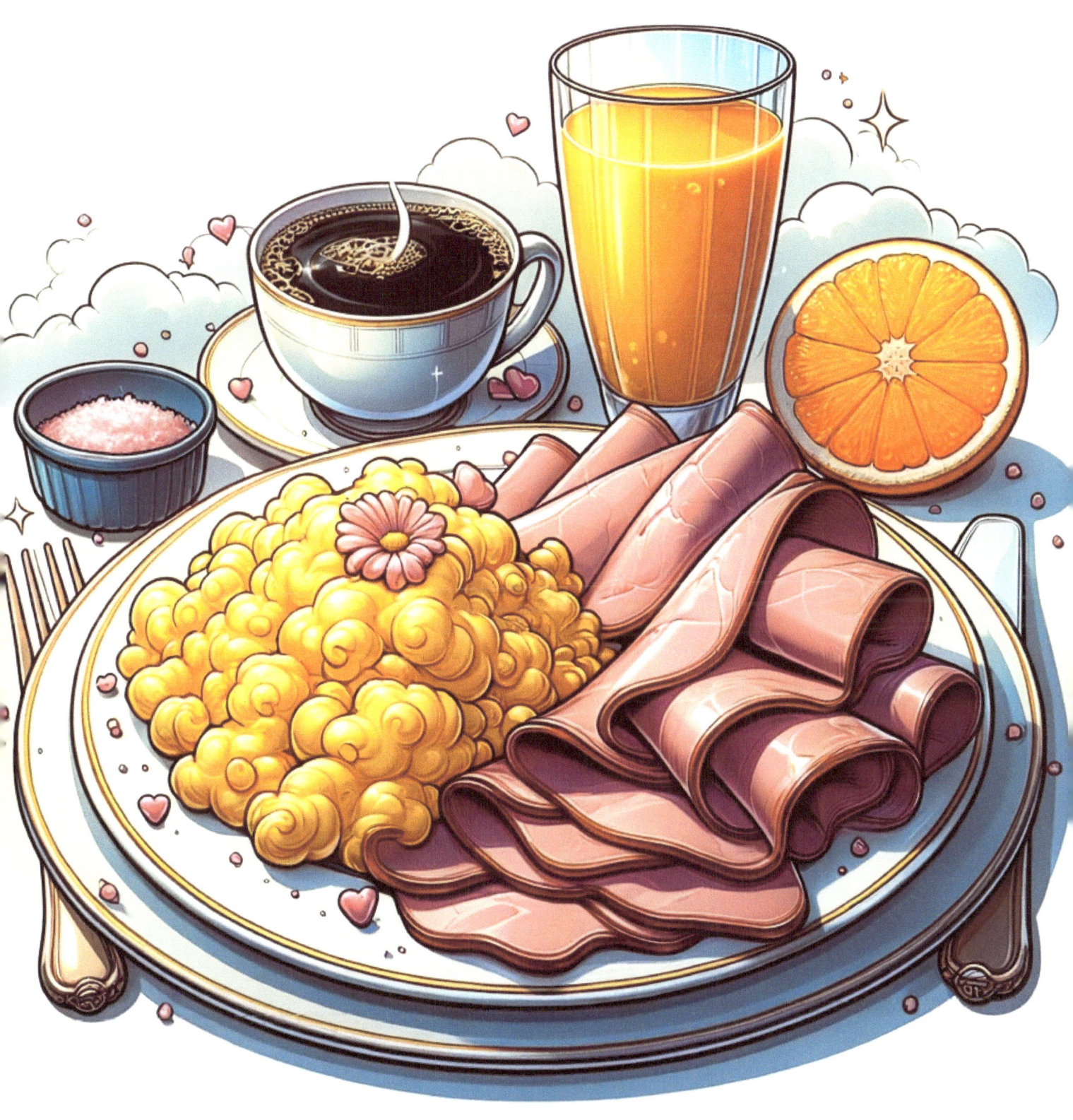

PROMPT

Create a cartoon digital illustration of a beautiful Sunday brunch plate, featuring fluffy pancakes, perfectly cooked eggs (sunny-side up), and crispy bacon. Alongside the main items, include a glass of orange juice and a cup of steaming coffee. The plate should also be adorned with various brunch fixings like slices of fresh fruit, a small bowl of berries, and a generous drizzle of maple syrup over the pancakes. The setting is designed to be festive and playful, with decorative garnish around the plate to enhance the ambiance. The illustration style should be playful and charming, capturing the essence of a delightful Sunday brunch, making it visually appealing and inviting.

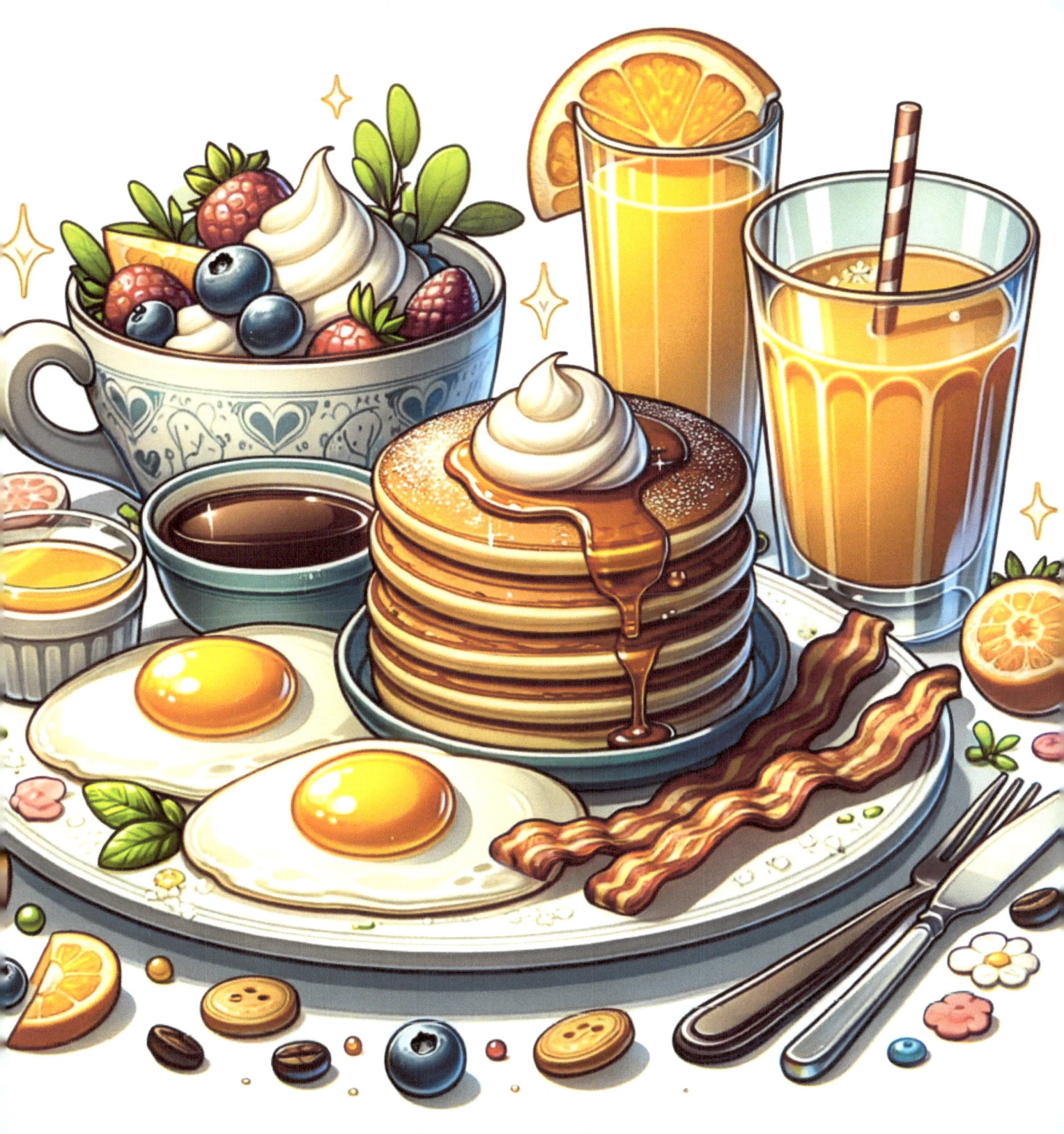

PROMPT

Create a cartoon digital illustration of a Sunday brunch plate featuring strawberry and blueberry crepes. The plate should showcase delicate, thin crepes filled with fresh strawberries and blueberries, topped with a light dusting of powdered sugar. Accompaniments include a glass of orange juice and a cup of steaming coffee, with small bowls of extra strawberries and whipped cream on the side for added flavor. The setting is cheerful and inviting, without any specific holiday decorations, focusing on the deliciousness of the crepes. Small decorative cut bananas can still be included around the plate. The illustration style remains playful and charming, capturing the essence of a delightful Sunday brunch with strawberry and blueberry crepes.

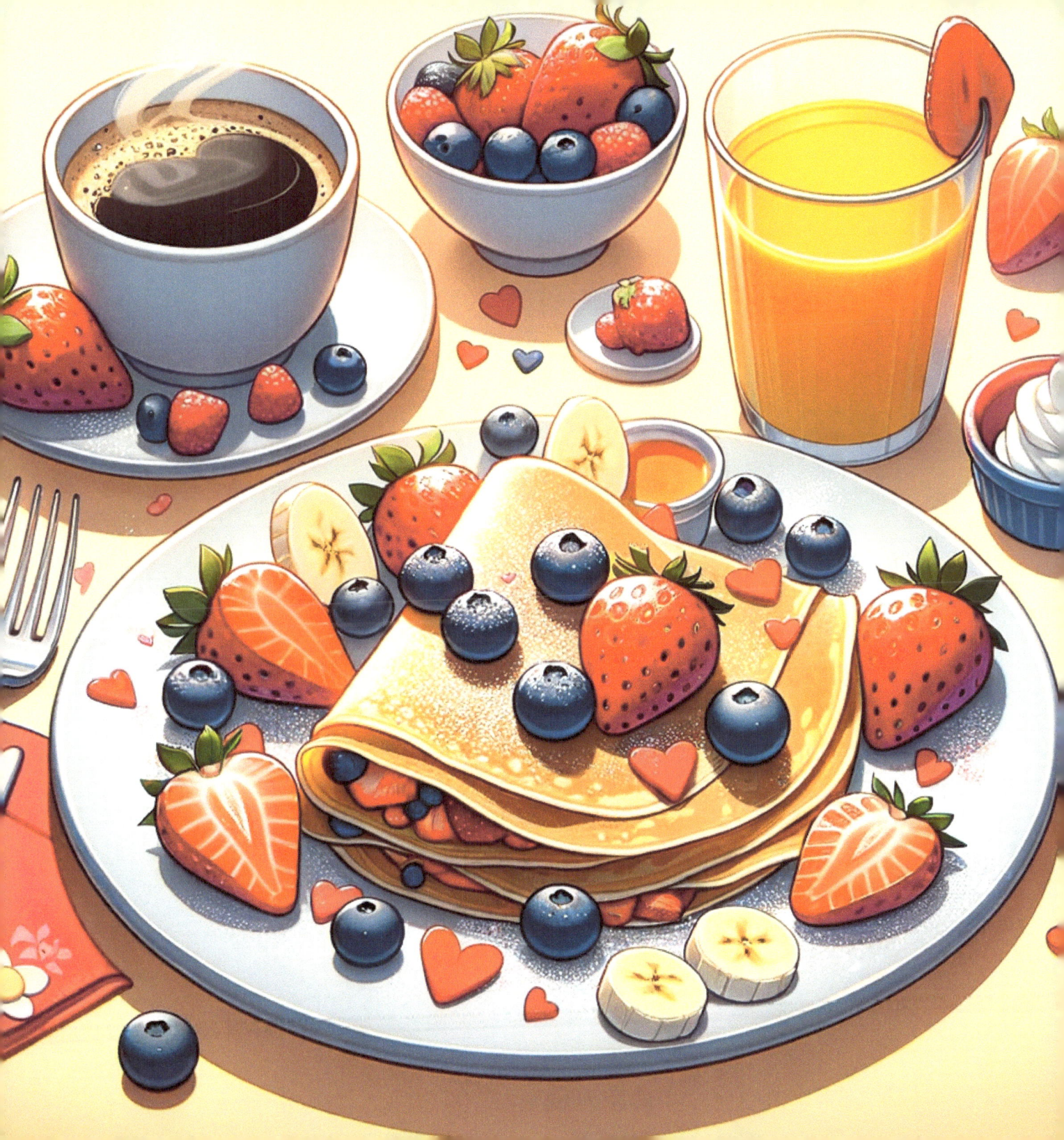

PROMPT

Recreate the cartoon digital illustration, now specifically adding an actual plate of fruit and cheese to the scene with the tall glass of hot cocoa with marshmallows and a bowl of hot cereal or oatmeal. Ensure the hot cocoa is rich and creamy, visible through the clear glass mug, topped with several fluffy marshmallows. The cereal, served in a cute bowl, should look appealing. The added plate should contain a variety of fruits and assorted cheese, placed prominently in the composition to enhance the cozy, inviting atmosphere of a winter breakfast. The background remains white to focus attention on the details of the breakfast items, creating a perfect ensemble for a warm winter treat. The illustration style is playful and charming, capturing the essence of a complete and cozy winter breakfast scene.

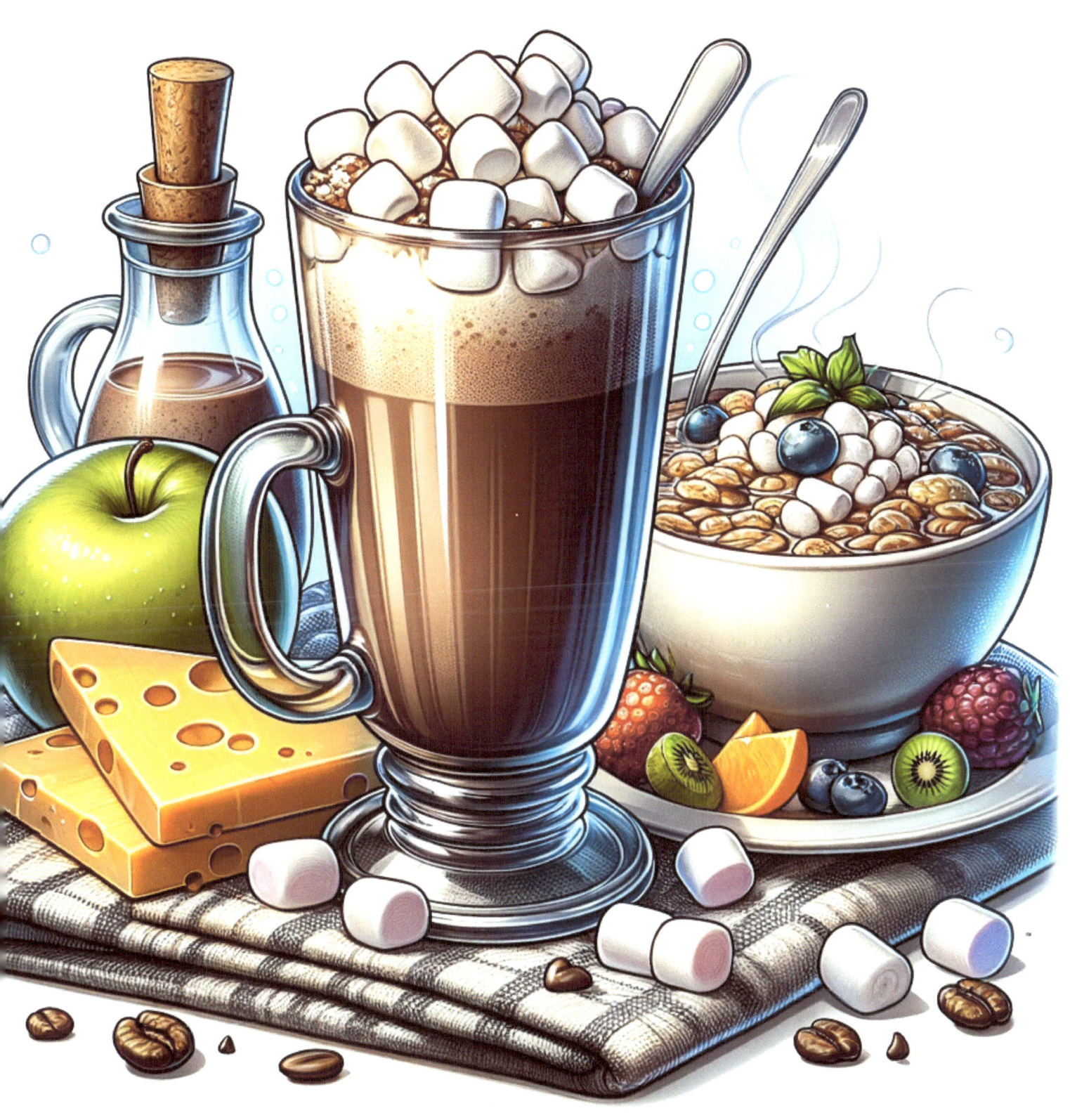

PROMPT

Create a cartoon digital illustration of a beautiful Sunday brunch plate featuring hearty waffles and perfectly cooked sausage, along with a glass of orange juice and a cup of steaming coffee. The plate should also include slices of fresh fruit, a small bowl of berries, and a drizzle of maple syrup over the waffles. The setting is designed to be festive and romantic, with a playful theme, including small decorative berries around the plate. The illustration style should be playful and charming, effectively capturing the essence of a delightful Sunday brunch with waffles and sausage. The overall scene should convey a sense of joy and indulgence, perfect for a romantic Sunday morning.

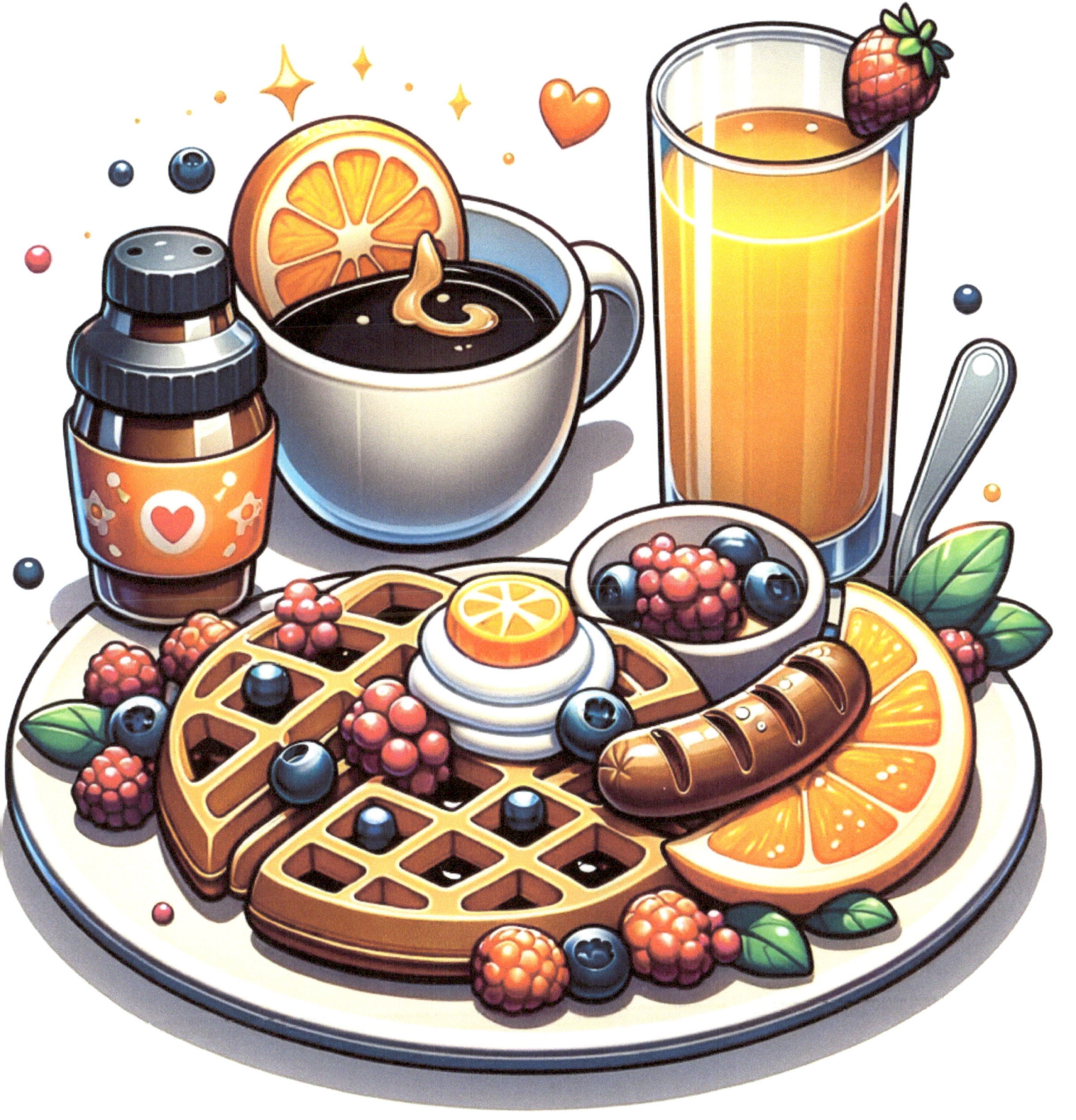

PROMPT

Create a cartoon digital illustration of a Sunday brunch plate featuring a perfectly cooked steak and a perfect omelet, along with a glass of orange juice and a cup of steaming coffee. Accompanying the main items, include brunch fixings like grilled tomatoes, a small bowl of spinach, and some toast on the side. The setting should be festive and fun, with small decorative garnishes around the plate. The illustration style is playful and charming, capturing the essence of a hearty Sunday brunch with steak and eggs. The scene should convey the indulgence and enjoyment of a classic Sunday brunch.

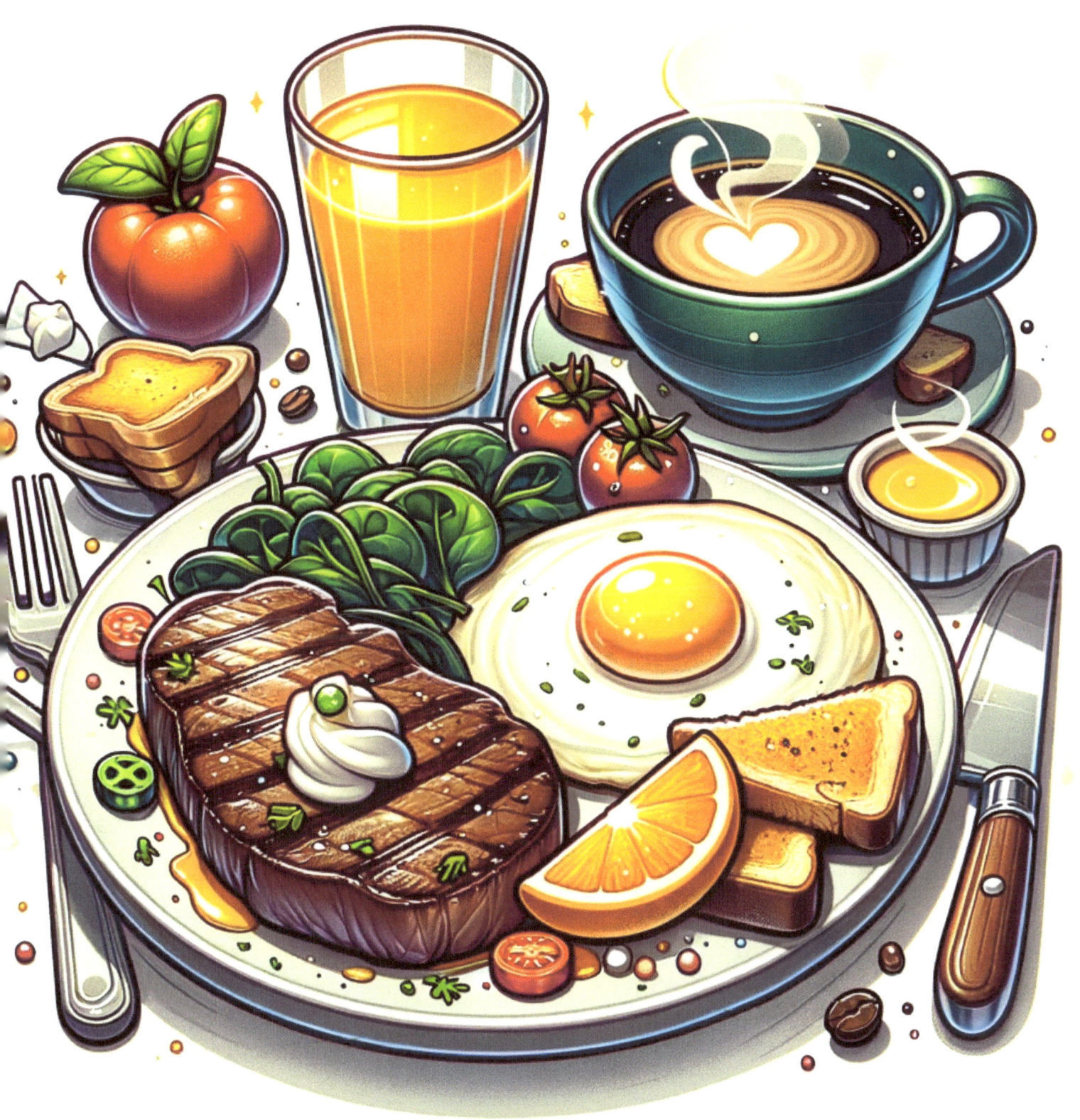

PROMPT

Create a cartoon digital illustration of a modern brunch plate featuring avocado toast topped with perfectly poached eggs. Include a side of mixed greens and a cup of artisan coffee, set against a backdrop of a chic and minimalist café atmosphere. The illustration should be vibrant and fresh, highlighting the healthful and trendy nature of the meal. The style should be playful and charming, capturing the essence of a contemporary and enjoyable brunch experience in an urban setting.

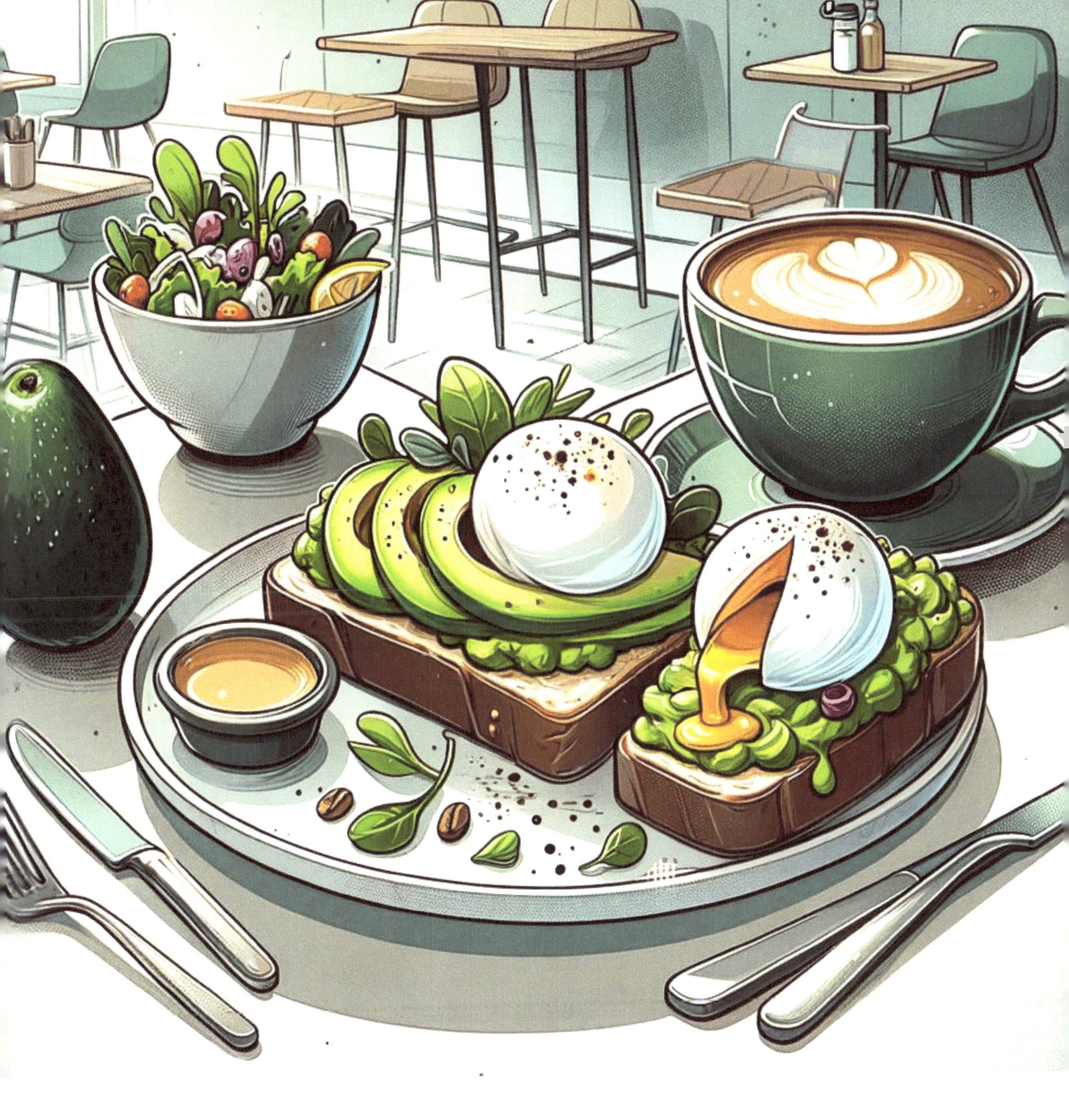

PROMPT

Illustrate a decadent brunch plate of French toast topped with caramelized bananas and a generous drizzle of caramel sauce, accompanied by a cup of cappuccino. The focus should be solely on the plate and the cup, without any background scene, to highlight the details and deliciousness of the dish. The style should be playful and charming, emphasizing the textures and rich colors of the caramelized bananas, the golden French toast, and the frothy cappuccino.

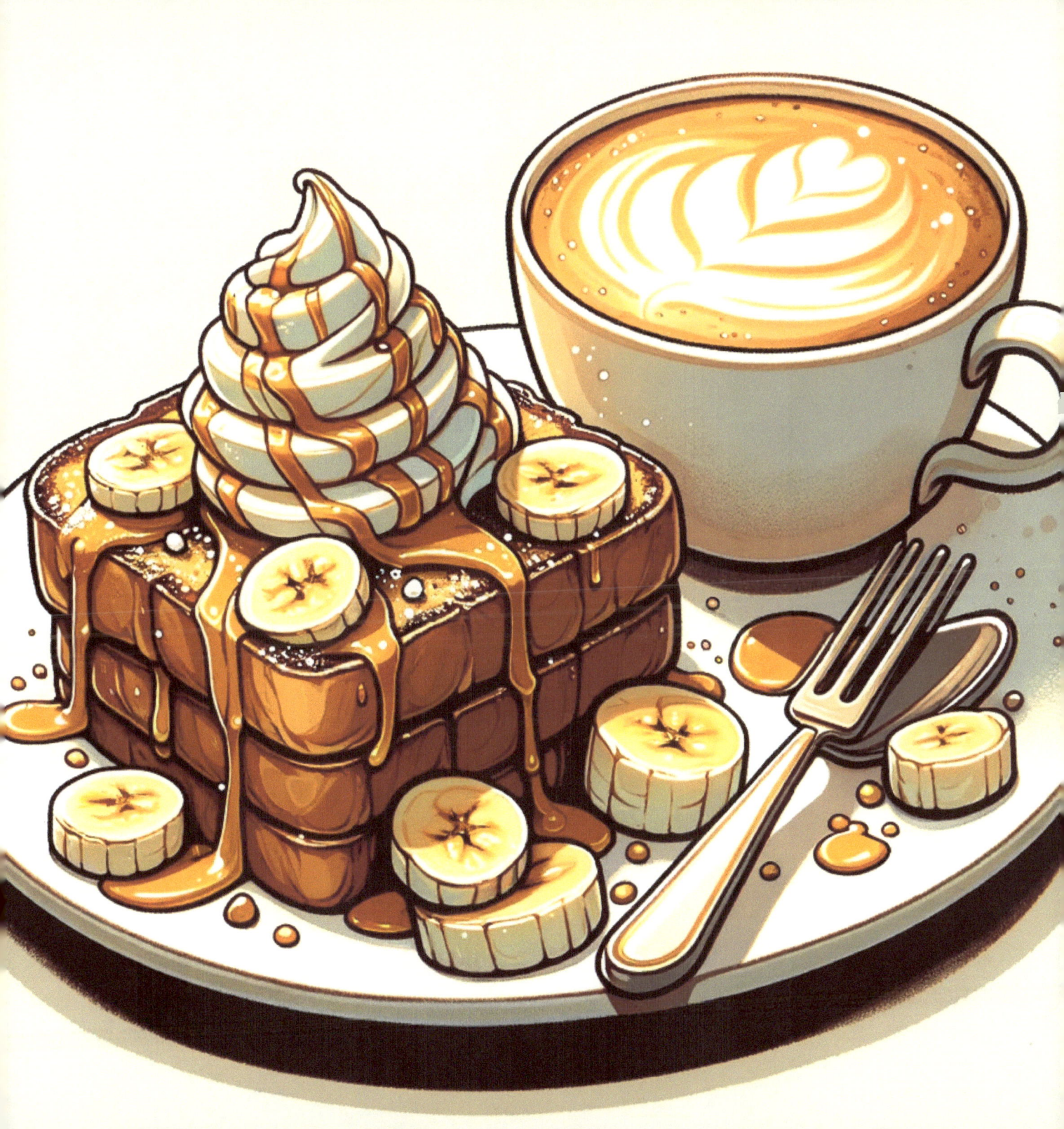

Bonus Prompts

1. **Shakshuka with Sourdough Bread:** Create a vibrant and spicy illustration of a skillet of shakshuka, featuring poached eggs in a tomato and pepper stew. Serve it with slices of crusty sourdough bread and a scene that captures the warmth and spices of the Mediterranean.
2. **Vegan Smoothie Bowl:** Depict a colorful vegan smoothie bowl topped with slices of banana, kiwi, berries, and granola. Include a glass of detox green juice and a peaceful garden setting to highlight a health-focused and refreshing brunch option.
3. **Huevos Rancheros:** Create an illustration of a vibrant plate of huevos rancheros with sunny-side-up eggs, avocado slices, and salsa on a corn tortilla. Include a side of refried beans and a chilled margarita, set in a sunny Mexican patio for a festive brunch atmosphere.
4. **Croissant Sandwich with Ham and Cheese:** Craft a cartoon depiction of a buttery croissant sandwich filled with ham, cheese, and greens. Accompany this with a fruit salad and a sparkling water, set in a quaint Parisian sidewalk café.
5. **Granola Yogurt Parfait:** Illustrate a layered granola yogurt parfait with layers of yogurt, mixed berries, and granola. Include a side of honey and a tranquil morning setting with a view of the sunrise, emphasizing a light and healthy start to the day.

Plus More

1. **Bagels with Lox and Cream Cheese**: Illustrate a Sunday brunch scene with a plate of bagels, generously topped with lox, cream cheese, capers, and red onion slices. Accompany this with a glass of fresh-squeezed orange juice and a cozy, inviting breakfast nook setting, capturing the essence of a leisurely weekend morning.
2. **Belgian Waffles with Berries and Whipped Cream**: Craft a cartoon depiction of a plate of Belgian waffles piled high with fresh berries and a dollop of whipped cream. Include a side of maple syrup and a latte art coffee, set in a sunny outdoor brunch setting that's playful and colorful.
3. **Classic English Breakfast**: Create an illustration of a full English breakfast plate, featuring eggs, bacon, sausages, baked beans, grilled tomatoes, mushrooms, and toast. The setting should evoke a traditional English pub with a cozy and warm atmosphere, emphasizing the hearty nature of the meal.
4. **Spinach and Feta Omelette with Artisan Bread**: Depict a gourmet brunch plate with a fluffy spinach and feta omelette, served alongside slices of warm artisan bread. Add a mimosa and a rustic kitchen table setting to convey a homey yet sophisticated Sunday brunch vibe.
5. **Blueberry Pancakes with Honey and Nuts**: Illustrate a stack of blueberry pancakes, drizzled with honey and sprinkled with crushed nuts. Accompany this with a side of bacon and a cup of black coffee, set against a backdrop of a bustling city café.

NOTES

www.ingramcontent.com/pod-product-compliance
Lightning Source LLC
Chambersburg PA
CBHW060837290526
45792CB00006BB/1966